VANITA'S DEDICATION

This book is dedicated to all my grandchildren

KRISTIN'S DEDICATION

To my amazing daughters Sage and Vi-yen

ACKNOWLEDGEMENTS

Many thanks to:

Kristin Blackwood
Mike Blanc
Kurt Landefeld
Paul Royer
Sheila Tarr
Jennie Levy Smith
Carolyn Brodie
Elaine Mesek

Ivan's Great Fall
VanitaBooks, LLC
All rights reserved.
© 2009 VanitaBooks, LLC

Text by Vanita Oelschlager.
Illustrations by Kristin Blackwood.
Design by Mike Blanc.

Printed in China.
Hardcover Edition ISBN 978-0-9819714-1-4
Paperback Edition ISBN 978-0-9819714-2-1

www.VanitaBooks.com

IVAN'S GREAT FALL

POETRY *for* SUMMER *and* AUTUMN

from GREAT POETS *and* WRITERS *of the* PAST

BY

VANITA OELSCHLAGER

ILLUSTRATION BY

KRISTIN BLACKWOOD

VanitaBooks, LLC

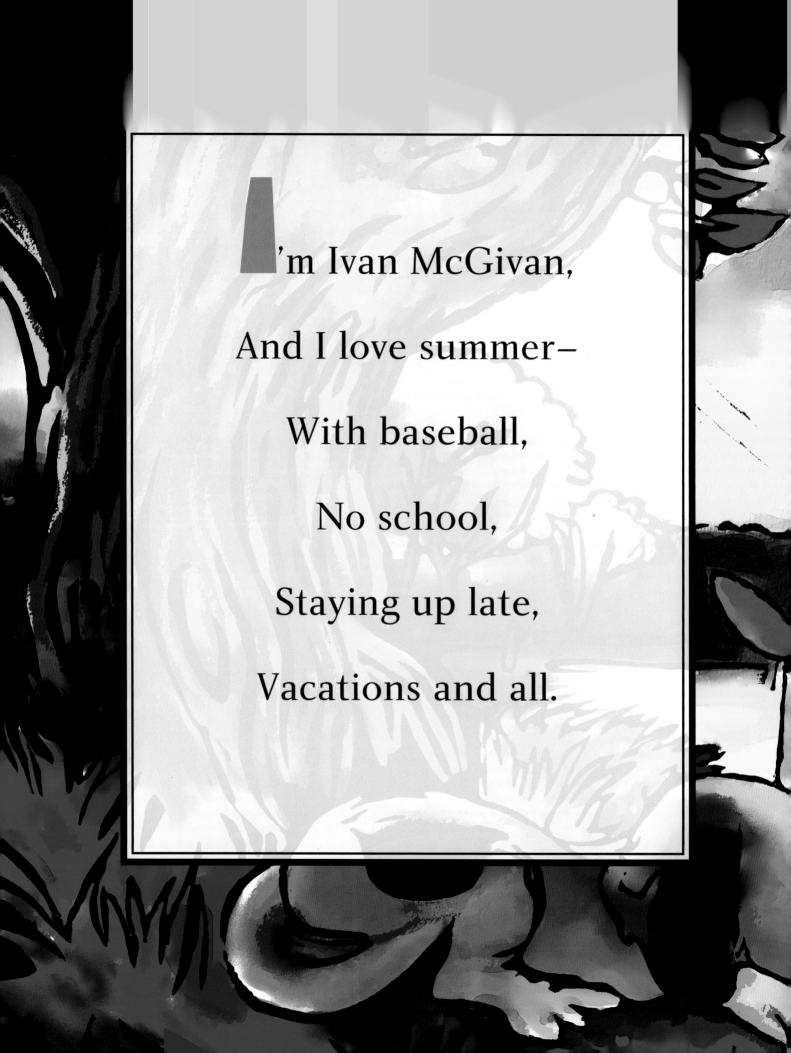

I'm Ivan McGivan,

And I love summer—

With baseball,

No school,

Staying up late,

Vacations and all.

I don't mind the heat.

There are so many reasons.

I wish all year was summer,

My favorite season.

I love to rise in the summer morn
When the birds sing on every tree.

Blessings on thee, little man,
Barefoot boy, with cheek of tan!

To hear the Blackbird, Cuckoo, Thrush,
or any bird in song . . .

Trees are lending a shelter from the sky.

Somewhere hearts are light,
and somewhere men are laughing,
and somewhere children shout;
But there is no joy in Mudville–

Mighty Casey has struck out.

How beautiful is the rain!

After the dust and heat,

In the broad and fiery street . . .

So near you are, summer stars.

In summer
when all the sky is clear and blue
and I should like so much to play
I have to go to bed by day.

'Tis the last rose of summer

Left blooming alone . . .

The nuts are getting brown;

The berry's cheek is plumper,

The rose is out of town.

And still more,
later flowers for the bees,
Until they think
warm days will never cease.

Give me juicy autumnal fruit,
ripe and red from the orchard.

In September, acres of birds
spotting the air going south.

In fall the outside will be
Orange and yellow and brown.
I will see my school friends
Once again
When I take the school bus
Into town.

I do like pumpkins
All carved to scare,
And Halloween,
And leaves in big piles
Everywhere.

Summer is almost gone.

And Fall will come.

It always does.

IVAN'S GREAT FALL

POETRY for SUMMER and AUTUMN

from GREAT POETS and WRITERS of the PAST

BIBLIOGRAPHY

Lines in orange were used for the illustrations.

William Blake wrote:
The School Boy *(excerpt)*

I love to rise in the summer morn
When the birds sing on every tree
The distant huntsman winds his horn,
And the sky-lark sings with me.
O! What sweet company!

*William Blake lived from 1757-1828. He was an English poet, painter and printmaker. His poem, "The School Boy" is from **Songs of Experience**, written in 1794.*

Vanita Oelschlager wrote:
Ivan's Great Fall *(beginning)*

I'm Ivan McGivan,
And I love summer–
With baseball,
No school,
Staying up late,
Vacations and all.

I don't mind the heat.
There are so many reasons.
I wish all year was summer,
My favorite season.

John Greenleaf Whittier wrote:
The Barefoot Boy *(excerpt)*

Blessings on thee, little man,
Barefoot boy, with cheek of tan!
With thy turned-up pantaloons,
And thy merry whistled tune;
With thy red lip, redder still
Kissed by strawberries on the hill;
With the sunshine on thy face,
Through thy torn brim's jaunty grace;
From my heart I give thee joy, –
I was once a barefoot boy!

John Greenleaf Whittier lived from 1807-1892. He was an American poet. He wrote "The Barefoot Boy" in 1855.

William Henry Davies wrote:

When on a Summer's Morn

When on a summer's morn I wake,
And open my two eyes,
Out to the clear, born-singing rills
My bird-like spirit flies.

To hear the Blackbird, Cuckoo, Thrush,
Or any bird in song;
And common leaves that hum all day
Without a throat or tongue.

And when Time strikes the hour for sleep,
Back in my room alone,
My heart has many a sweet bird's song –
And one that's all my own.

*Poet William Henry Davies lived from
1871-1940. He was born in Wales.*

Emily Bronte wrote:

Moonlight, Summer Moonlight

'Tis moonlight, summer moonlight,
All soft and still and fair;
The solemn hour of midnight
Breathes sweet thoughts everywhere,

But most where trees are sending
Their breezy boughs on high,
Or stopping low are lending
A shelter from the sky.

And there in those wild bowers
A lovely form is laid; Green grass and dew-
steeped flowers
Wave gently round her head.

*Emily Bronte lived from 1818-1848. She was a
poet and a novelist.*

Ernest Lawrence Thayer wrote:

Casey at the Bat *(excerpt)*

The outlook wasn't brilliant for the Mudville
nine that day:
The score stood four to two, with but one
inning more to play.
And then when Cooney died at first, and
Barrows did the same,
A sickly silence fell upon the patrons of the
game.

A straggling few got up to go in deep despair.
The rest
Clung to that hope which springs eternal in
the human breast;
They thought, "If only Casey could but get a
whack at that –
We'd put up even money, now, with Casey at
the bat."

[. . .] Oh, somewhere in this favored land the
sun is shining bright;
The band is playing somewhere, and somewhere
hearts are light,
And somewhere men are laughing, and somewhere children shout;
But there is no joy in Mudville - mighty Casey
has struck out.

*Ernest Lawrence Thayer wrote "Casey at the Bat"
for The San Francisco Examiner on June 3, 1888.*

Henry Wadsworth Longfellow wrote:
Rain in Summer *(excerpt)*

How beautiful is the rain!
After the dust and heat,
In the broad and fiery street,
In the narrow lane,
How beautiful is the rain!

How it clatters along the roofs,
Like the tramp of hoofs
How it gushes and struggles out
From the throat of the overflowing spout!

Across the window-pane
It pours and pours;
With a muddy tide,
Like a river down the gutter roars
The rain, the welcome rain!

*Henry Wadsworth Longfellow lived from 1807-
1882. He was an American Poet and Educator.*

Carl Sandburg wrote:
Summer Stars

Bend low again, night of summer stars.
So near you are, sky of summer stars,
So near, a long arm man can pick off stars,
Pick off what he wants in the sky bowl,
So near you are, summer stars.
So near, strumming, strumming,
So lazy and hum-strumming.

*Carl Sandburg lived from 1878-1967. He was
a reporter, author and poet. He was born in
Galesburg, Illinois. This poem was written in
1922.*

Robert Louis Stevenson wrote:
Bed in Summer

In winter I get up at night
And dress by yellow candle-light.
In summer quite the other way,
I have to go to bed by day.

I have to go to bed and see
The birds still hopping on the tree,
Or hear the grown-up people's feet
Still going past me in the street.

And does it not seem hard to you
When all the sky is clear and blue
And I should like so much to play
To have to go to bed by day?

*Robert Louis Stevenson lived from 1850-1894. He was born in Scotland. He was a writer and poet. This poem, "Bed in Summer" is from a group of poems in **A Child's Garden of Verses**.*

Thomas Moore wrote:
'Tis the last Rose of Summer *(excerpt)*

'Tis the last rose of summer
Left blooming alone;
All her lovely companions
Are faded and gone:
No flower of her kindred,
No rose-bud is nigh,
To reflect back her blushes,
O give sigh for sigh.

Thomas Moore lived from 1779-1852. He was an Irish poet, singer, songwriter and entertainer.

Emily Dickinson wrote:
Autumn

The morns are meeker than they were,
The nuts are getting brown;
The berry's cheek is plumper,
The rose is out of town.
The maple wears a gayer scarf,
The field a scarlet gown.
Lest I should be old-fashioned,
I'll put a trinket on.

*Emily Dickinson lived from 1830-1886. She was an American poet. This poem, "Autumn" is from **Nature 28 – Autumn**.*

Walt Whitman wrote:

Give me the Splendid, Silent Sun *(excerpt)*

Give me the splendid silent sun, with all his beams full-dazzling;
Give me juicy autumnal fruit, ripe and red from the orchard;
Give me a field where the unmow'd grass grows;
Give me an arbor, give me the trellis'd grape;
Give me fresh corn and wheat - give me serene-moving animals, teaching content;
Give me nights perfectly quiet, as on high plateaus west of the Mississippi, and I looking up at the stars;

*Walt Whitman lived from 1819-1892. He was an American poet, essayist, journalist and humanist. This poem, "Give me the Splendid, Silent Sun" is from his collection of poems, **Leaves of Grass** that he published the first time himself, in 1855.*

Carl Sandburg wrote:

Falltime *(excerpt)*

What is there for you in the birds, the birds, the birds crying down on the north wind in September, acres of birds spotting the air going south?
Is there something finished? And some new beginning on the way?

*Carl Sandburg lived from 1878-1967. He was a reporter, author and poet. He was born in Galesburg, Illinois. This poem, "Falltime" was part of a longer poem, **Cornhuskers**, which he wrote in 1918.*

John Keats wrote:

To Autumn *(excerpt)*

To bend with apples the moss'd cottage-trees,
And fill all fruit with ripeness to the core;
To swell the gourd, and plump the hazel shells
With a sweet kernel; to set budding more,
And still more, later flowers for the bees,
Until they think warm days will never cease,
For summer has o'er-brimm'd their clammy cells.

John Keats lived from 1795-1821. He was one of the great English poets. This is part of his poem, "To Autumn."

Vanita Oelschlager wrote:
Ivan's Great Fall *(conclusion)*

In Fall the outside will be
Orange and yellow and brown.
I will see my school friends
Once again
When I take the school bus
Into town.

I do like pumpkins
All carved to scare,
And Halloween,
And leaves in big piles
Everywhere.

Summer is almost gone.
And Fall will come.
It always does.

VANITA OELSCHLAGER

Vanita Oelschlager is a wife, mother, grandmother, former teacher, caregiver, author and poet. She was named "Writer in Residence" for the Literacy Program at The University of Akron in 2007. She is a graduate of Mount Union College, Alliance, Ohio, where she is currently a member of the Board of Trustees.

KRISTIN BLACKWOOD

Kristin Blackwood is an experienced illustrator whose other books include: *My Grampy Can't Walk, Let Me Bee, What Pet Will I Get?, Made in China, Big Blue and Ivy in Bloom.* She has a degree from Kent State University in Art History. In addition to teaching and her design work, Kristin enjoys being a mother to her two daughters.

ABOUT THE ART

Kristin's illustration is a blending of techniques, beginning with traditional block prints, cut in linoleum, and printed in black on white stock. The images were converted to digital format through flatbed scanning. Watercolor layers were added using Corel® Painter™ and Adobe® Photoshop® computer software for digital illustration. The result, *Ivan's Great Fall*, is a delightful visual journey.

PROFITS

All net profits from this book will be donated to charitable organizations, with a gentle preference towards serving people with my husband's disease – multiple sclerosis.